COOKING WITH MAMMA J

THE BEGINNERS GUIDE TO FEEDING THE SOUL

BY JACKIE HILTON